Queen's Wicked Tongue

QueenAmina

The Dedication

This book is for all the ones that never gave up on me in my journey. The loyal ones that always and forever believed in the Queen and knew that I would once again rise to my fullest sunshinest QueenAmina ever. The true ones beyond a shadow of a doubt had my back to the fullest... this one's for you!!

I love and appreciate you all

LOVE QUEEN AMINA

Copyright 2023 QueenAmina
Cataloging in Publication Data
QueenAmina
Queen's Wicked Tongue/QueenAmina, A book of poetry written by QueenAmina
Some characters and events in this book are fictitious. Any similarity to real persons, living or dead, is coincidental and not intended by the author.
Front cover design by Jewel R. Jordan, CEO of J R Media Chicago LLC, jrmediachicago.com
Printed and bound in the United States of America First printing 2023

Queen's Wicked Tongue

Dedication Poem by QueenAmina

We thank you God for our daily bread
Not just for the food we are fed
But for the nourishment in our head
Knowing that we cannot find it staying in bed
We Thank you for everything you've ever said
I will be eternally grateful until the day that I am dead
Listening quietly and the negativity fled
letting your love continuously spread
We appreciate everything you ever did
I've been inlove with you since I was a kid
There is no greater love than yours
I have your presences coming out of all my pores
With you I will always sore
Together we always score
There is only ceilings no floors
My dear God
I feel your presence inside
From you I never have to hide
And now I speak anyway I want to with pride
You have been the only father that I have ever had
And I feel blessed to call you Dad
I know you know my heart even if my action is a sin
Thank you Father for allowing me to WIN
AMEN, AMEN & AMEN!!!!!!!!

G.R.A.C.E

G.R.A.C.E

I have the world on my shoulders even though I carry it with grace
It's heavy as shit, but I don't wear the pain on my face
I'm moving so fast
Standing in one place
I'm in pieces
These words are my releases
I need to gift the world my Positivity
It shall build internally
But negativity
Because I kept it in me
To scared of opinions
Forgetting I'm God's minion
And I'm on a mission
So if you not wit me cooking in the kitchen
Adding to the pot
The major ingredients and what not
Building up this legacy
That's motivating me
The books, businesses and buildings
Name ringing in all the surroundings
Houses in other countries
This will be my REALITY
I walk hard and strong
Moving to the best of my own song
That's why I smile no matter what I've been through
There has always been a light in my tunnel
Now you know
No matter how heavy my shoulders grow
Ima carry on with dignity and grace
I been won this shit, it was never no race!!!!

"Everytime is the First Time"

"Everytime is the First Time"

If I saw you all over again
One glance...one smile, one grin
It would still be you that I would want
With a hint of flirt and a bit of taunt
Smiling with my eyes
Watching the sun rise
Kisses on the forehead
Believing in the words you said
If I bumped into you on the street
A casual chance meet
It would still be you that would make me
shy Nervous every time you pass by
It would be nice I bet
For us to watch the sun set
Kisses on your cheek
When we greet
I know when you're near
I blush from ear to ear
That's how I know in entirety
Absolute true certainty
If I ever saw you again
I couldn't just be your friend
You're the ripples and the waves
You make my thoughts misbehave
Kisses on your chin
And I'm a kid again
Lost in a daze
Thinking of all the ways
I would be elated
If our paths were no longer separated
Seeing you everyday from your head to
your toes Ending everyday with soft kisses
on your nose
I'll see you again
In the morning
Waking up to your face
Your loving embrace
Being in your arms even under your neck
Coming home from a long day smelling
like sweat It's you I love and have forever
Looking at you everyday has been my
pleasure That why seeing you everyday
feels like a dream It's more than I imagine
more than it seems

Knowing that I'll see you all over again
One glance...one smile, one grin
I hurry up and sleep so a new day can begin Because I love waking up to a kiss on my chin

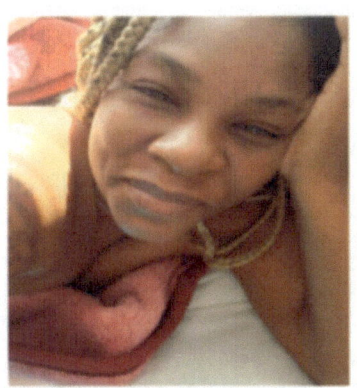

6 FIGURES

6 FIGURES

I hate the song it's raining men
I don't wanna hear it again
It's raining six figure
Niggas
They pockets are bigger
I ain't no gold digger
But I need a few commas and zeros
Before my legs unfold
Sick of those broke wanna fucks
That just want dick sucks
Only rain on me
If your account can take care of the economy

It's raining six figure niggaz
And their dicks are bigger
Catch one and you're the winner
Some can even cook dinner
I ain't no salad-eating Queen
I'm the woman of your dreams
So say hallelujah when you catch one like me

We're diamonds simply royalty

Some treat you with respect
I know that's something most don't expect
They love real hard
Take away your pains and scars

Making sure anything you need is done Keeping it loyal because you're their only one

It's raining educated six figure niggaz That really knows how to treat her Better get out there and catch you one

They'll be gone by the time the rain is done

WITH ME

WITH ME

I don't know where to begin
All I can say is with me in your life... You Win!!!!

I'm good for that ass like Scott
I'm better than dessert I hit the spot
I got your back like glue
With someone like me you won't know what to do

I give my full attention
Love and a ection
Communication
With a positive indentation

I'm a diamond I the ru
Ain't nobody like me I'm built Ford tu
I'm soft as butter
Ain't no better lover
I fight and I shoot
Bonnie & Clyde screaming GIMMIE DA LOOT!!!!

I'm a bad girl
But I can be your world
Loyal and sexy
No one can test me
Strong enough to take on anyone
Submissive enough to know where I end & you begun
I can suck the life from your soul

Having you ready to say to have and to hold
Looking good even old
Pussy so wet the bed will never be cold
I want your mind
And your time
I can make you feel amazing every day
I'll never lie to you so believe what I say
Are you up for the task
Can you handle all this ass

Can you tame
My brain
Can you ease my pain
Let this body drive you
insane Are you up for the
journey Emotionally
Pleasantly
For the rest of eternity

PHILLY USED TO BE!

PHILLY USED TO BE!

I come from the 215
When it was totally live
Now the cops ain't shit
White people on drugs in a fit
They bombed the MOVE movement

For that they better repent
We used to have the D.A.R.E
Now them fuckers better not come near me
Then Philly got 267
And more black people are in heaven
Mayor John Street
Openly did drugs fuck discreet
They got cops climbing in windows
Taking our children to where nobody knows
Philly used to be the city of Brotherly Love
Water, Ice, Cheesesteaks, and all above
Now the motherfucker is 445
The whole shit done took a dive
I miss being in the fireplug with neighbors

Borrowing sugar for favors
Making moves together as a family

Everyone living so happily
Philly, Philly...Philly where I am from
Now it's not even a place I ever want to come

I drive through
I don't go to
It changed for the worse
Everyone I loved dead, gone in a Hearse

I'm PHILLY born and raised
But damn MY Philadelphia has seen better days

Niggaz Quiere

Niggaz Quiere

Men that be on my top
Are quickly not
When they learn about this brain
It's wild and not tame
They be looking at my hips
Underestimating my lips
My verbiage
Cuts threw cartilage
The things manifesting
in my cerebral cortex
Will have a weak man stretched
They have these intermittent dreams
Of their grand schemes
Fitting me nicely into their plan
When they don't even understand
I'm here for me
Cute and hella sexy
You are a bonus
But I'm focused
You think a text
Will get you sex
I'm not that, baby boy
I'm for real...nobodies toy
 You want me to be on your top
I'm not
I won't be
This is a guarantee
I'm for you
As an equal
I got your back
Carry the ghat
But if you come at me
wrong
It won't last long
So I hope I've addressed

your concerns
In layman's term
You have thoughts in your head
However you're misread I'm not something
you've conjured
What you've pondered
The images you've pulled upon
seeing my social media
I'm so much more than
any idea
I'm Queen Gangsta of the
streets
Freak in the sheets
Common sense on fleek
Knowledge game Ima geek
Keep it discreet
I fight and shoot,
Yup...I'm complete
So as long as you're on
my top
Non stopped
You won't get dropped
Stepped over with
flip-flops
Everything with me is
two way
Hear what I say
Me for you and vice
versa
Now there is no need for
guessing you know all about
her

BOY BYE

BOY BYE

How you want me on your top
Calling, reaching out to you stopped
Now that you remember that I exist
And I don't wanna fuck wit you and you're pissed

Get a fucking life
Your should have thought twice
Before you disappear
Now for you I don't give not one single care
I moved on to loving myself
Obtaining generational wealth
I give a damn about me
Now you can kiss this BIG, SOFT BOOTY
Don't think about me and call months later
I've been snatched up by something greater
You stopped speaking to me for no reason
Showing me you were just a season
Now you on my phone
Talking about you all alone
Well too bad for you
Ima keep doing what I do
That's shining bright like a diamond or should I say star

Can't hear you I've gone too far
I've grown into what I'm meant to be
Too damn bad you couldn't see
What you had or what I was on my way to be

Better hold onto the memories

Oh so sad that you lost the Queen

Close your eyes and I'll appear in your dreams

I won't give you another thought though

Just like the river I will always flow
Now stop reaching out talking about hey how you been

Because I'm laughing at you with a devilish grin

Bye boy

Fucking enjoy

Whatever you thought was better

I'm done when I type this last letter.

Queen's delight

Queen's delight

We stepped out on to the concrete
It felt like clouds beneath our feet
I woke up on my own private jet
Living as good as it gets
I looked over to see your face
My heart begins to race
As we embrace
Crazy orgasmic chase
Intense pace
That taste
Your face
Below my waist
Let's go
Start slow
Deep strokes
Grab my throat
Put your hand in the ark of my
back Just like that
Hurt me good, that painful
pleasure Keep going until you hit
gold- treasure Deep strong strides
Now it's my turn to ride
Mounting you like a cowgirl
About to make your toes curl
Make you speak in tongue
Definitely about to make you cum
Slowly pulsating and grinding
Body winding

My hands on your chest
You gently squeezing my breast
Tickling my nipples with your fingertips
Mouths pressed together lip to lips
Ass cheeks clapping
Hands smacking
No end in sight
Pleasing you with all my might
Next position
Let's hit submission
The night has just begun
This transition is only the third one
Hold on for the ride
I have a lot more to give inside
Toys, whipped cream, chocolate syrup honey and ice I got what we need to keep everything flowing nice

Through it all

Through it all

I always smoke alone
In my own thoughts in my own zone
I always stand on my own two
I never needed you
I added a boo
It was just us, not a few
That's why I never pass my Dutch
Don't even look and definitely don't
touch Most pass it to the left
Most def
That's only if we ..brown
Ten toes down
You gotta be deep in my circle
To catch my purple
Haze
And get dazed
Float high with the Queen
If you know what I mean
When I passed and you said "I'm
good"
"I guess I could"
I smiled because you knew
It should always be us two
I didn't need to smoke alone
Because you're home
And when the smoke cleared
It was only you standing there

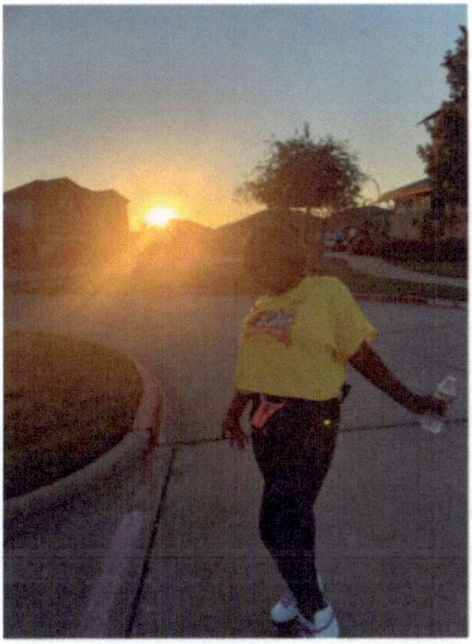

*The end is
The beginning*

<u>The end is The beginning</u>

This wicked tongue
Has just begun
Beyond intelligent
No more being hesitant
If you don't like it then leave
I can't stand still there is much to achieve
No more knocking at the door
I'm kicking it open taking all that I deserve and
more Motivation behind the smile on my face
Let's go!! No time to waste!!

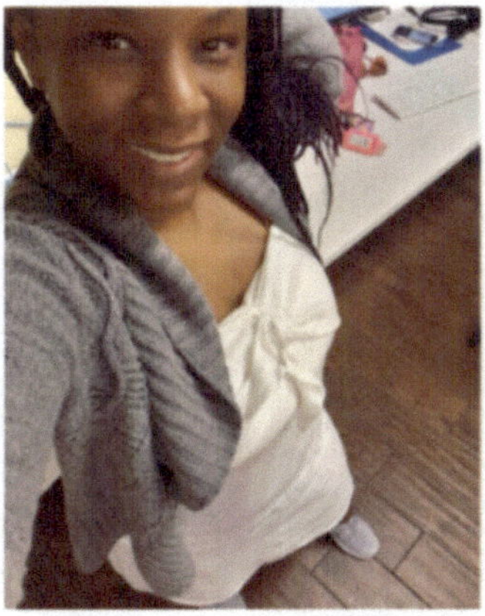

Home is
where you are

Home is where you are

If you wanted me naked in your arms
With all my invigorating charms
You would have stayed
Together we'd be on our knees prayed
That we're going to treat each other right
Pussy delicious and tight
Sex is a fight
Holding on with all our might
I don't bite
I don't see anyone you're the only one in my
sight Treating you as my one and only
Always got your back you'll never be lonely
Riding you to sleep
Always ready no reason to creep
Fucking you to death and sucking you awake
Never getting enough, oh heaven sake
Making your body shake
Orgasims like an earthquake
Taken all the dick
Because I'm your chick
Your wife your Queen
Living life like a dream
Or so it seems
Making this pussy cream
Getting money
With my honey
Making moves

We'll always be in a groove
Sexy when we step out
Your the man, mad clout
I'm the boss Princess
Together totally blessed
We're going to treat each other right
Pussy delicious and tight
Sex is a fight
Holding on with all our might
I don't bite
I don't see anyone you're the only one in my sight Making each other moan
Living on a powerful throne
In our zone
Together.....now that's home

GIRL BYE

GIRL BYE

Shorty you want to know
How he went from Captain save a hoe
To oh hell no
Simple... my pussy is on glow
I'm stating facts
I'm all that
You look like your mama pushed and the doctors shoved

You got a face nobody loved
I'm self made
Face look like I'm only a decade
Body on GOD DAMN
Ass like ohhhhh man
I'm grace
Everything in place
I don't chase
I won the race
I'm Queen Amina Show-It-Well
I'm always "She Pass" never fail
I'm self made
Extra paid
Do it all my the grace of God
Its hard but I make it look like a glide
I'm Everything to the right people
I'm always above you girl, never equal
I never need saving
Sometimes misbehaving
It feel good to be so bad
I'm happy in my skin that's why you mad

I'm always going to be sunshine

Aging like very fine wine

SO....
Look but don't touch

I'm always going to be too much

That's why he no longer wanna save a hoe

Because with me he can grow

I'm not a want I'm a need

His soul, I'll always feed

I'll always be head of the class

It's my heart and brains, not just my

ass

No one can compare

That why he's here

Not there

Adios my dear

Yes I speak Espanol

And I'll be his to have and to hold

Hearing about me

Hearing about me

Fake friends I can so without

Talking behind your back...no doubt

I rather sit back and listen to the stories

That people tell me about me

They're quite entertaining

I hear I'm dead..nothing else remaining

These fantastic tales

Make my confidence swell

I hear, how I'm down and irreconcilable

I live this life every and these gossips are unrecognizable

I wonder who believes them

They sound just dumb

I mean hell, if I've made it there and back

Nothing I say or do should sound wack

People wanna be

Me...

When I'm just trying to survive

Thanking my God for everyday that I'm alive

They say that I make it look easy

Saying yes all the time just to please me

Not know how hard it is daily

Making sure my four children aren't failing

Running to crazy jobs at all hours

Just trying to hold it all together with all my powers

Living from check to check

Breaking my back and my neck

Sprained my ankle and broke my arch

Still making time to meditate and practice my art

Easy my ass

Kids mad they gotta take out the trash

Calling me a slave driver

Because I'm piecing shit together like Magiver

I'm the glue and the tape

Can't let them know that I got raped

Gotta stay strong listening to the fables

If I let the lies and bullshit hurt me then I won't be able

To

Make my dreams come true

My reality

My destiny

I know words aren't supposed to hurt, but they do

And I will attack you

Hurt people, actually hurt people

So go tip toe

And whisper over there in the dark

Sometimes I'm a bitch and you don't want her to bark

It's all fun and games

Fingers pointed, no one taking blame

What shame

Because I fight and I got great aim

You, you and you

Don't know what I've been through

The fire was hot, the clouds where cold

I guess I'll be hearing & laughing at these stories about me until I'm old

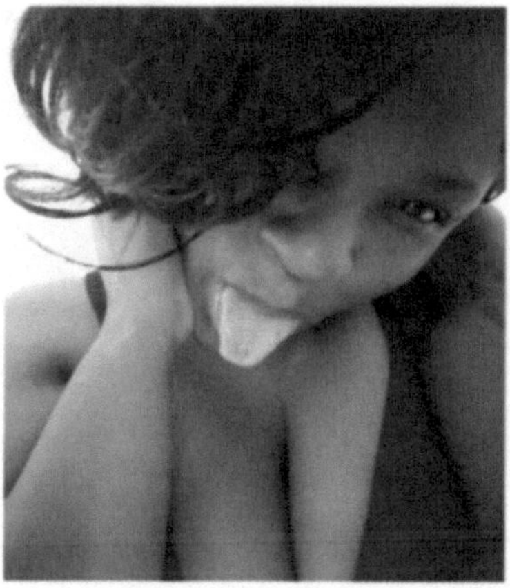

Fake niggaz

Fake niggaz

The wolf in sheep's clothing as struck again
He's ever so sweet with a devilish grin
He is educated and wise
With hypnotic eyes
You'll get stuck in his word play
Falling in love with everything he say
He strong and hugs like you need
He's amazing he can't be a bad seed
He's disassociate
But acts appropriate
You'll be lost with the first meet
Thought knowing him would be a treat
His scent knocks you o your feet
Moved from my seat
Now that's a great feat
The wall I build without trying he sure did defeat
I just knew that I met my match
Can date, chill, talk, touchy without the over attach Being lost in that moment
Feeling so innocent
Guards down
No stopping us now
It was what I needed
Two years waiting...depleted
And as fast as you could say "I'm home"
From your cell phone
He's gone

Nothing since "we must do this again"
A lie to go along with the sin
Still have your scent on my shirt
Smiling at the way you flirt
No hard feelings
Memories of feet on ceilings
A moment needed at the time
Mixed feelings about how your path crossed with mine Wish I could slap your face
Because you think with below your waist
Hoping we cross paths again
So that I can punch you in your chin
Wishing we didn't get lost in the moment
So you better repent
I want to run you over with my truck
To show you that I don't give a fuck
I hate you pretend to be nice
Just to get a slice
Pretend to care
Just to get some derriere
Act like you want part of someone's life
Fake like you want a wife
Wolves in sheep's clothing
Looking for ass only, no betrothing
Run quickly ladies these fools ain't shit
But they will lick your clit
Quick
The wolf in sheep's clothing as struck again
He's ever so sweet with a devilish grin
He is educated and wise
With hypnotic eyes

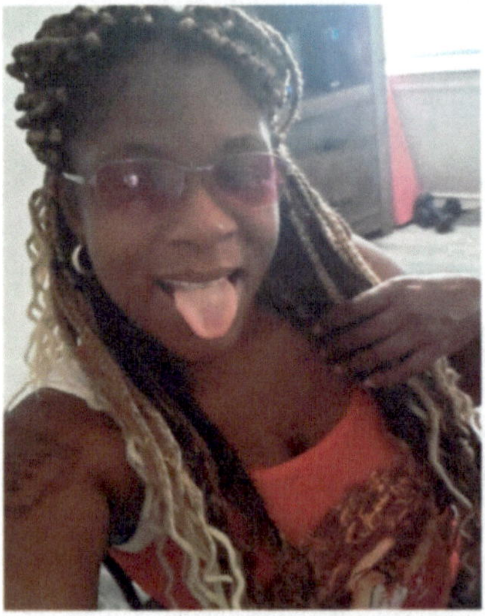

Madam Queen Goat Dragon

Madam Queen Goat Dragon

Fuck the goat I'm the dragon
Intimidating from my dome to all this wagon
Don't give a shit about your emotions
Even if your tears flood like oceans
I'm La Jefa, the one in charge if the situation
So don't try my patience
The me... you knew is gone
Evolved.... as life moved on
You stood still in time
Now look at you as part of this rhyme
I'm the motherfucking dragon now
And Ima need you.. to bow down
To this crown
The new inspiration around
From the looks of it... I'm long overdue
So move out the way, I'm coming through
I've sat and watched
But it's time to take it up a notch
A few notches or whatever it is
This is now my biz
Now sit down and catch these blessings
Learn these lessons
Ima give you plenty of jewels
Just follow these rules
Stop tweaking in these fucking streets
And start tweaking between them sheets
Put some damn clothes on and leave something to the imagination

It's a better males mental illumination
Stop being so revealing
It's a little more appealing
Take it from the the dragon
I'm the shit ..yeah I'm bragging
I'm wanted in every state
By every man with a heart rate
And every woman with a pulse
And anything else you come across
Ima a goat by birthday right
December 26 is my night
Capricorn
And you don't want the horns
So fall in line
I'll tell you what I have in mind
For this global take over
With me as the controller
Let's undoubtedly take our place
In this crazy ass rat race
Make them all pick up the pace
Us.... they'll have to chase
To the finish line
Because we're never behind
Now allow me the MadamQueenGoat Dragon
To lead you ladies in that fashion

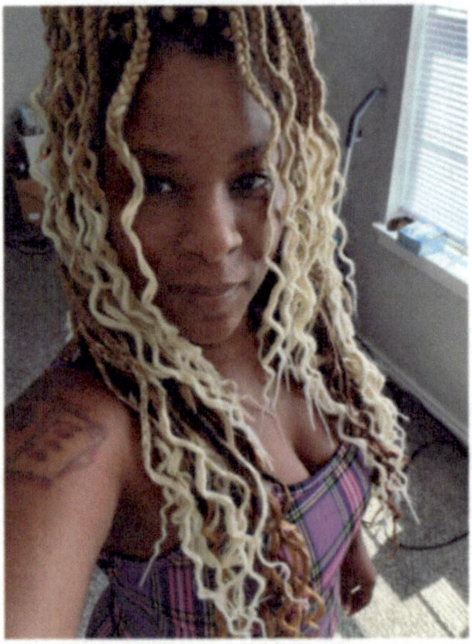

Phenomenally

Phenomenally

I am me
Phenomenally
I'm a prodigy
And Ironically
No one thought that I could be
As outstandingly
Iconically
Let alone so amazingly
Articulately
Expressively
Fancifully
I'm just being me
So Phenomenally
Beautifully
Educatedly
Fantastically
Gratefully
Building my body
Mind and spiritually
Staying Holy
Praying daily
Protected Godly
Asking for forgiveness and taking
liability Confessing sins as me
Owning it Phenomenally
Moving humbly
Never hesitantly
Confidentially

Fabulously
Gallantly Proudly
Wonderfully As
me Phenomenally

QueenAmina (c) 2023

I am Love Love
is Me

Please don't test me!!

Please don't test me!!

Love, you think you can break me down...
Nope you're a clown...
You think you can destroy my spirit ....
Nope I can bear it.......
You think you can play with my mind.....
Nope, you can kiss my behind.....
Goodbyes, from all your lies,
no more cries,
Not one more tear,
not one more care to spare!!
Bye-bye now..,,
have no time to frown...
the world keeps going...
Ima keep glowing...
my mind will keep growing.
And you...
lol, any who!!!
You think you can destroy my heart,
nope you don't get to do that part.,
You think you can play with my emotions.... such a

funny notion.......

You actually think it's a game..,
what a lame....
This poem needs no name....
You know that I'm speaking to you...
can't say your name anyways that might have been a lie

too....
because that's all you truly do.
Is LIE...

wishing you would just die!!!
You're a fraud...
but your effort I applaud.....
You tried it....
but quickly showed me that you ain't shit......,
living above your means....
always trying to remain seen....
selling everyone a fucking dream!!!!
Boy bye,
all you know how to do is LIE!!!!
That's why in the end ...
you'll have to buy a friend.....
again you tried it....
but you don't fit....
You're emotionally dead....
Mentally misled.....
Not sexual enough in bed.....
and always trying to convince someone of the BullShit in your head!!!!!
You don't even know who you are....
So surprised you got this far.....
YOU THOUGHT YOU COULD HURT THE QUEEN......
Don't you know I play for God's team....
I'm a sunbeam....
A Rich and a Poor man's dream.....
I am definitely what I seem!!!!
I walk in my truth....
First one to confess at the booth!!!!
Boothang you thought you could stop my stride....
never because I walk with pride......

I'm always down to ride......
and in God I confide !!!!!!
You thought you were strong enough to take me down......
If the shit wasn't so funny I would frown......
Ima give you some advice....
with God's children you should play nice......
or simple think twice......
you don't want to start a war.....
this one isn't like any you've ever fought before!!!!!
Remember No one can take me down....
you fucking lying assclown!!!!!
I am God's daughter...
and this is for YOU, in that fucking order!!!!!!

Queen Amina © 2019
Bonus Throwback poem

The Best In Urban Fiction & Poetry!

Show-IT-Well Publications

267-551-0124

aminashowell@showitwellbooks.webs.com

ORDER FORM

NAME OF BOOK	#OF BOOKS	PRICE OF BOOK	TOTAL
*ENTER THE MIND OF THE QUEEN (POETRY)		$15.00	
*THE QUEEN HAS SPOKEN (POETRY)		$15.00	
INNER SOUL (POETRY)		$15.00	
*IN THE HEART OF THE QUEEN (POETRY)		$15.00	
*QUEEN SURVIVED (POETRY)		$15.00	
*IF SOME WISHES CAME TRUE (NOVEL)		$19.99	
WISHES ACTUALITY (NOVEL)		$19.99	
*WHERE THE LOYALTY LYES #1 (NOVEL)		$19.99	
*WHERE THE LOYALTY LYES #2 (NOVEL)		$19.99	
*WHERE THE LOYALTY LYES #3 (NOVEL)		$19.99	
WILL'S DESTINYY (NOVEL)		$19.99	
*QUEENIE'S SECRET (NOVEL)		$19.99	
THE QUEEN PIN (NOVEL)		$19.99	

*Lessons Through Time (Novel by Madafah Lindsey)		$17.99	
*QUEEN'S WICKED TONGUE (POETRY)		$16.00	

Please note the following

FOR Autographed copies or BULK orders
Cash payments are strongly discouraged.

Payments for books can be made through:

PayPal
{aminaqb@yahoo.com}

Zelle
 {aminaqb@yahoo.com}

CashApp
{$QueenAmina26}

To place any bulk orders please feel free to email
{showitwell1@gmail.com}

For personal Autographed copies please include what you would like written with your payment. Thank you for keeping Show-It-Well Publications in your thoughts and letting us fulfill your reading needs

Sincerely,
Queen Amina
CEO Show-IT-Well Publications

COPYRIGHTS

All rights reserved. No part of this book may be reproduced, stored, or transmitted by any means—whether auditory, graphic, mechanical, or electronic—without the written permission of both publisher and author, except in the case of brief excerpts used in critical articles and reviews. The unauthorized reproduction of any part of this work is illegal and is punishable by law.

Show It Well Publications

CEO Queen Amina

Made in the USA
Columbia, SC
26 May 2024